LANGSTON
HUGHES

THE VOICE OF HARLEM

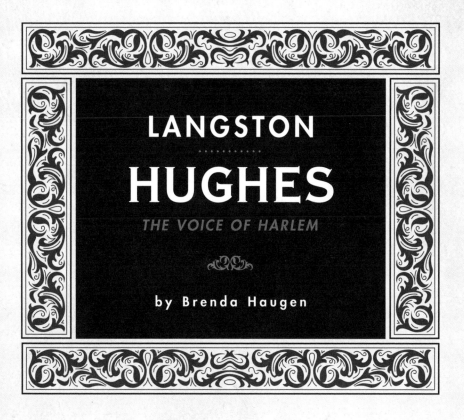

LANGSTON
HUGHES
THE VOICE OF HARLEM

by Brenda Haugen

Content Adviser: Marcellus Blount, Ph.D., Associate Professor,
Department of English and Comparative Literature,
Columbia University

Reading Adviser: Rosemary G. Palmer, Ph.D.,
Department of Literacy, College of Education,
Boise State University

COMPASS POINT BOOKS MINNEAPOLIS, MINNESOTA

Compass Point Books
3109 West 50th Street, #115
Minneapolis, MN 55410

Visit Compass Point Books on the Internet at *www.compasspointbooks.com*
or e-mail your request to *custserv@compasspointbooks.com*

Editor: Jennifer Van Voorst
Lead Designer: Jaime Martens
Photo Researcher: Marcie C. Spence
Page Production: Heather Griffin, Bobbie Nuytten
Cartographer: XNR Productions, Inc.
Educational Consultant: Diane Smolinski

Managing Editor: Catherine Neitge
Creative Director: Keith Griffin
Editorial Director: Carol Jones

To Auntie Ann. Your love and support mean the world to me! BLH

Library of Congress Cataloging-in-Publication Data
Haugen, Brenda.
  Langston Hughes: the voice of Harlem / by Brenda Haugen.
     p. cm. — (Signature lives)
  Includes bibliographical references and index.
  ISBN-13: 978-0-7565-0993-4 (hardcover)
  ISBN-10: 0-7565-0993-9 (hardcover)
  ISBN-13: 978-0-7565-1860-8 (paperback)
  ISBN-10: 0-7565-1860-1 (paperback)
  1. Hughes, Langston, 1902–1967—Juvenile literature. 2. Poets,
American—20th century—Biography—Juvenile literature. 3. African
American poets—Biography—Juvenile literature. 4. Harlem
Renaissance—Juvenile literature.
I. Title. II. Series.
PS3515.U274Z6637 2006
818'.5209—dc22   2005003256

Photographs reprinted by permission of Harold Ober Associates Incorporated.

From THE WEARY BLUES-BOOK COVER
by Langston Hughes, copyright reprinted
by permission of Alfred A. Knopf, a Division of Random House Inc.
Used by permission of Alfred A. Knopf, a division of Random House, Inc.

From THE WAYS OF WHITE FOLKS-BOOK COVER
by Langston Hughes, copyright reprinted
by permission of Alfred A. Knopf, a Division of Random House, Inc.
Used by permission of Alfred A. Knopf, a division of Random House, Inc.

Signature Lives

MODERN AMERICA

Starting in the late 19th century, advancements in all areas of human activity transformed an old world into a new and modern place. Inventions prompted rapid shifts in lifestyle, and scientific discoveries began to alter the way humanity viewed itself. Beginning with World War I, warfare took place on a global scale, and ideas such as nationalism and communism showed that countries were taking a larger view of their place in the world. The combination of all these changes continues to produce what we know as the modern world.

Table of Contents

1 SPEAKING OF RIVERS

ໜ∽≪∾ຈ

Langston Hughes stared idly out the window of the train. Traveling from Cleveland, Ohio, to his father's home in Toluca, Mexico, he had a lot of time for day-dreaming. As he watched the countryside roll by, he thought about his past and his hopes for the future.

Crossing the Mississippi River outside of St. Louis, Missouri, however, Langston's mind wandered to the river. He thought about what the Mississippi meant to black people in the United States. In the days of slavery, being sold down the Mississippi River—farther into the heart of slave territory—was the worst thing many slaves could imagine. He thought about the rivers of Africa, such as the Congo and the Nile, and the black people whose lives are entwined with them. He also thought about

In his poetry, Langston Hughes wrote of the experience of being black and American.

The Mississippi River ranks as the second-longest river in the United States. The Missouri River holds the title of the longest. The Mississippi runs 2,340 miles (3,744 kilometers) from Northwest Minnesota to the Gulf of Mexico.

his father, who seemed to hate black people, even though he was one himself. His father believed they took what they got without trying to make better lives for themselves. Langston and his father didn't see eye to eye on this and many other issues.

That day, as the train crossed the Mississippi River, Langston's thoughts first collided and then came tumbling out. He reached for an envelope and wrote down a line: "I've known rivers." The rest of the poem came quickly, and after about 15 minutes, the words held the places they'd likely stay.

"The Negro Speaks of Rivers," written on a train on the back of an envelope, would become the first poem Hughes would publish. It would also become one of the most popular of the many poems he would ever write. But for now, 19-year-old Langston tucked it away with his things as he traveled.

Langston Hughes would have a rocky summer with his father, but he had endured worse. A lonely childhood and an unstable adolescent home life had prepared him for the worst life had to offer—and it had helped him nurture big dreams. At the top of the list was making a name for himself as a writer.

I've known rivers:
I've known rivers ancient as the world
and older than the flow of human blood
In human veins!
My soul has grown deep like the rivers.
I bathed in the Euphrates when dawns
were young.
I built my hut beside the Congo and
it lulled me to sleep.
I looked upon the Nile and raised the
pyramids above it.
I heard the singing of the Mississippi
when abe Lincoln went down
to New Orleans,
and I've seen its muddy bosom
turn all golden in the sunset.
I've known rivers:
ancient, dusky rivers.
My soul has grown deep
like the rivers.
From memory to read
on radio show —
Langston Hughes

Hughes copied down his poem "The Negro Speaks of Rivers" before reading it on the radio.

Hughes continued to write and publish, and as his career and fame grew, he used his own life experiences to guide his writing. He had a lot of experiences to write about. Hughes traveled the globe, visiting museums and places other tourists frequent, but he found more satisfaction in seeking out the forgotten people—the poor and downtrodden who lived in the shadows. These people inspired him.

Hughes inspired budding poets through his readings and lectures.

Much of what Hughes wrote served to show what life was like for a black man in his day. He hoped his work would show black people they should be proud of themselves and help white people understand what it felt like to be a black person in the United States in the first half of the 20th century. Hughes' poems celebrated the beauty of African-American speech and used the rhythms of black music to deliver their powerful messages. He put strong ideas into words that people of every background could understand.

Over the course of his career, Langston Hughes published 16 books of poems, three collections of short stories, two novels, about 20 plays, musicals, and operas, eight children's books, three history books, two autobiographies, and newspaper and magazine articles too numerous to count.

His words, and sometimes his presence, sparked both protest and praise. But his mission was simple. He just wanted to shed light on injustices he saw. He wanted people to think and feel. He wanted his words to bring equality for all people. Although he wouldn't live to see such a day, Langston Hughes never quit trying. ❧

2 A LONELY CHILDHOOD

Chapter

ꙮ

Born James Mercer Langston Hughes, Langston never went by the name James. Langston was born in Joplin, Missouri, on February 1, 1902. His father, also named James, left his family shortly after Langston's birth. He found life in the United States to be too difficult for a black man in the early 1900s. Trained as a lawyer, James soon realized that he wouldn't be allowed to have a profitable practice in the United States because of laws that discriminated against blacks.

James wanted to go to Cuba or Mexico where he had a chance to make a good living, but Langston's mother, Carrie, didn't want to go. When James became successful, however, Carrie, Langston, and Carrie's mother, Mary, traveled to Mexico so that

Langston Hughes spent his childhood in the Midwest, but he never lived anywhere for very long.

Langston Hughes, age 3

Carrie and James could try to make their marriage work. At the time, Langston was 5 or 6 years old.

The attempt to reunite their family didn't last long, though. When Langston and the women arrived in Mexico, an earthquake shook the ground. That proved to be enough of Mexico for Carrie. The women took Langston and headed right back to the United States.

For much of her life, Carrie always seemed to be off looking for a better job and a better place to live. Langston spent much of his youth being shuffled back and forth among relatives and friends. The year Langston started elementary school, though, he was living with his mother in Topeka, Kansas.

Carrie had a year of college and was able to get a job as a stenographer for a black lawyer named Mr. Guy. The job didn't pay much, and all Carrie could afford was a room over a plumbing shop, where she lived with her young son. A little stove not only gave Carrie a place to cook—one pot at a time—but it also provided the apartment's heat. Since Carrie didn't have money to buy wood for the stove, Langston spent part of every day after the area stores closed looking for empty boxes shopkeepers had thrown away. Carrie burned the boxes in the stove for heat. Though the apartment wasn't fancy, at least it was close to her workplace. Carrie didn't own a car and there was little money for bus fare.

Because their home was downtown, Langston went to school in the downtown district. No other black people lived in the area, and Langston was the only black student at the school. At first, school officials didn't want Langston to go to the downtown school. Langston remembered:

> *They wanted to send me to the colored school, blocks away down across the railroad tracks. ... But my mother, who was always ready to do battle for the rights of a free people, went directly to the school board, and finally got me into the Harrison Street School—where all the teachers were nice to me, except one who sometimes used to make remarks about my being colored. And after such remarks, occasionally the kids would grab stones and tin cans out of the alley and chase me home.*

In 1954, an elementary school in Kansas' capital city of Topeka drew the nation's attention. In a landmark case called Brown vs. the Board of Education of Topeka, the Supreme Court decided that racial segregation in public schools was unconstitutional.

But one white boy always stood up for Langston. Sometimes others also found the courage to follow his lead. Besides, Langston was a really nice person, and it was hard not to like him. The unfailing kindness of the one white boy, however, taught Langston not to judge people by their skin color.

"So I learned early not to hate all white people," he said. "And ever since, it has seemed to me that most people are generally good, in every race and in every country where I have been."

Langston's mother, Carrie Mercer Langston Hughes

Though she had little money, Carrie enjoyed the arts and wanted her son to appreciate them as well. She always found enough money to take Langston to the theater. She also loved books and spent time with Langston at the public library. He later said:

There I first fell in love with librarians, and I have been in love with them ever since—those very nice women who help

*you find wonderful books! ... The silence
inside the library, the big chairs, and long
tables, and the fact that the library was
always there and didn't seem to have a
mortgage on it, or any sort of insecurity
about it—all of that made me love it. And
right then, even before I was six, books
began to happen to me, so that after a
while, there came a time when I believed
in books more than in people—which, of
course, was wrong.*

As Langston prepared to enter the second grade,
he went to live with his Grandma Mary in Lawrence,
Kansas. Nearly 70 when Langston was born, Mary
came from French, Cherokee, and African ances-
tors. Aside from the fact that Mary's straight black
hair was long, many people said Langston looked a
lot like her. "She was a proud woman—gentle, but
Indian and proud," Langston later said.

Mary had been born a free person in North
Carolina, but her husband, Charles Langston, had
been the son of a slave. His mother, Lucy Langston,
had served as the housekeeper for Captain Ralph
Quarles, a Virginia plantation owner who was also
Charles' father.

Langston's grandmother on his father's side of
the family was the daughter of Silas Cushenberry, a
Jewish slave trader from Kentucky. His grandfather
was a Scottish man named Sam Clay, who was said

to be a relative of the famous American statesman Henry Clay.

Langston's Grandma Mary cherished her freedom, something not all people of black ancestry had when she was young. She went to college in Oberlin, Ohio, and married a free man named Sheridan Leary. They both shared the same values and wanted all people to be free. Sheridan gave his life for the cause. He died in the first night of the Harpers Ferry raid led by abolitionist John Brown. "My grandmother said Sheridan Leary always did believe people should be free," Langston said. He later recalled:

> *I remember once she took me to Osawatomie, where she was honored by President Roosevelt—Teddy—and sat on the platform with him while he made a speech, for she was then the last surviving widow of John Brown's raid.*

A radical abolitionist, John Brown planned to attack the United States arms store at Harpers Ferry, Virginia, in October 1859. He planned to take as many weapons as possible and give them to slaves. He hoped they then would rebel against slavery and fight for their freedom. Many of his men were killed in the battle for the arsenal, and Brown was captured the next day. He was convicted of treason and hanged.

After Sheridan's death, Mary met Charles Langston. They fell in love and married. After moving to Lawrence, Kansas, in the 1870s,

Mary and Charles welcomed the birth of their daughter Carrie, Langston's mother.

Charles never made much money, though he worked very hard. Along with farming, he ran a grocery store and got involved in politics. When he died, he had little to leave to his family. Life would always be a struggle for them. Some of Langston's earliest memories involve his grandmother worrying about how she would pay the mortgage on their home.

Langston's grandmother, Mary Sampson Patterson Leary Langston

An independent woman, Grandma Mary refused to work for other people. Still, she had to pay their mortgage and put food on the table. She earned money by renting out parts of her home to families or to students at the local university. Sometimes Mary and Langston ate little in order to save enough money to ensure they didn't lose their home. When times were especially tough, they'd even move in with friends and rent out the whole house in order to raise enough money for the mortgage.

Life with Grandma Mary proved to be sad and

lonely for Langston. On most days, Mary sat in her rocker and read the Bible. Sometimes, though, she'd read fairy tales or newspaper articles to her grandson. She also loved to hold Langston on her lap and tell him stories of the past—and she had lots of tales to tell.

As soon as Langston learned to read, however, he found comfort in books. While reading books, Langston could be anyone and travel anywhere on great adventures. His world was only limited by his imagination.

Though she could provide her grandson with few physical comforts, Grandma Mary loved Langston and taught him to be proud of who he was.

Langston attended the Pinckney School in Lawrence, Kansas.

When Langston was around 7, she took him to hear Booker T. Washington speak. Though Langston recalled little about what the man said, Washington made a huge impact on the boy, who was part of a crowd filled with both blacks and whites. "I was very proud that a man of my own color was the center of all this excitement," Langston remembered.

Born into slavery in 1856, Booker T. Washington grew up to become one of the most influential black leaders of his time. A teacher, Booker T. Washington founded the Tuskegee Institute, a school for black people in Alabama, and worked to promote harmony between blacks and whites.

Mary also introduced Langston to a new magazine called *The Crisis*. Edited by Dr. W.E.B. DuBois, the magazine was published by a fledgling civil rights group called the National Association for the Advancement of Colored People (NAACP). *The Crisis* brought attention to important black Americans and the issue of racism.

When Langston was 12, Grandma Mary died. He went to live with her friends James and Mary Reed. Though they weren't related to Langston, he still called them Uncle Reed and Auntie Reed, and he adored them with all his heart. "For me, there have never been any better people in the world," Langston said. "I loved them very much."

In 1913, street-cars shared the street with horses in Lawrence, Kansas.

Auntie and Uncle Reed didn't worry about money as much as Grandma had. Their small home near the railroad station was already paid in full, and there never seemed to be a shortage of food on their table. They both held regular jobs, too. Uncle Reed worked for the city placing sewer pipes. He also dug ditches. The Reeds also kept animals, including chickens and cows. Auntie Reed sold eggs and milk to the neighbors.

The Reeds treated Langston well, and he liked living with them. Along with helping complete chores around the house, Langston found outside jobs, too. He hunted for maple seeds, which he sold to the local seed store, and he delivered and sold newspapers.

Langston's first steady job came when he went into the seventh grade. At a hotel near his school, Langston kept the lobby tidy and cleaned toilets. For his hard work, he earned 50 cents a week.

He also found time for fun. On Saturdays, Langston went to see the University of Kansas football team play. He also went to movies. The woman who owned the movie theater, however, didn't like that Langston frequented her business. Soon she put up a sign that read "No Colored Admitted." Langston had dealt with Jim Crow laws before, and he didn't argue. Instead, he started going to the opera house and watching performances there. He went alone, but he still loved it.

When Langston turned 14, his mother sent for him. Langston would find himself in a new state, with a new family. New challenges loomed on the horizon, but he could hardly wait.

Jim Crow laws were designed to keep blacks and whites apart. Such laws made blacks and whites use different drinking fountains and public bathrooms and kept the races apart on buses and in train stations and other public places. The name Jim Crow came from a black character from a popular song in the 1830s.

3 HIGH SCHOOL

Chapter

❧∽❧

Langston could barely contain his excitement. He couldn't count the number of times he'd stood at the Lawrence depot and stared at the train tracks. They carried people around the country. They even led to the magical city of Chicago, Illinois.

Langston's mother, Carrie, waited for him in Lincoln, Illinois, a city between St. Louis and Chicago. She had married a man named Homer Clark. Together, they had a son, Gwyn. Having Langston with them would complete their little family.

Langston was excited to join his mother and the rest of the family. He'd dreamed of Chicago for a long time. In Lawrence, Kansas, Chicago seemed far away—a huge city filled with wonderful people and endless possibilities.

Langston (at left) was a popular student at his Cleveland, Ohio, high school.

Langston loved his new family, including Homer and Gwyn. It proved fun to have a little brother after growing up all alone with his grandmother.

Homer first worked as a chef, but grew tired of working in a hot kitchen. He'd often be on the road looking for other jobs. With World War I being fought in Europe, Homer easily found jobs in war-related industries. Factories scurried to fill overseas war orders at the war's start in 1914. Homer worked in steel mills and coal mines, but the jobs always came with a price. All the time away from home made him miss out on some important days in Langston's life. One of them included Langston's graduation from the eighth grade. Fourteen-year-old Langston had been chosen as "class poet," though he'd never really thought about writing before.

Langston remembered:

World War I lasted from 1914 to 1918. The fighting grew to include many countries, including the United States, but started with France, Great Britain, and Russia fighting Germany and Austria-Hungary. The assassination of Archduke Franz Ferdinand of Austria-Hungary on June 28, 1914, fueled tension among the countries and proved to be the spark that started the war.

> *They had elected all the class officers, but there was no one in our class who looked like a poet, or had ever written a poem. There were two Negro children in the class, myself and a girl. In America most white people think, of course, that all Negroes can sing and*

*dance, and have a sense of rhythm. So my
classmates, knowing that a poem had to
have rhythm, elected me unanimously—
thinking, no doubt, that I had some, being
a Negro.*

For graduation, Langston wrote a poem praising his teachers and his classmates. He'd never forget the roar of applause that followed his reading. "That was the way I began to write poetry," he said.

Carrie was proud of her son's honor. She fancied herself a poet and liked that her son showed a knack for the art, too. In fact, Carrie loved performing. One time, Langston remembered, he, Carrie, and another

Langston (left) was pleased to rejoin his family, which now included a little brother named Gwyn (front right).

little boy dressed up for a performance at a church in Lawrence. Carrie took the event very seriously. Langston, however, did not.

As Carrie performed her part of the work, Langston stood on stage rolling his eyes. People in the audience noticed and started to giggle. Carrie didn't know what was going on and increased her efforts at being dramatic. Langston stepped up his antics, too, acting as if he were in great pain. The crowd couldn't contain itself, and bursts of laughter erupted. At the end of the performance, a horrified and confused Carrie stood as the audience clapped and laughed at the same time. Langston later said:

> *When the program was over and my mother found out what had happened, I got the worst whipping I ever had in my life. ... Then and there I learned to respect other people's art.*

After finishing eighth grade, Langston moved with his family to Cleveland, Ohio, where Homer landed a good-paying job in a steel mill. Most of Homer's money, however, went toward rent. Landlords charged blacks two, three, or more times the rent they'd charge white people for the very same apartment.

Blacks possessed no power to complain. Thousands came from the South hoping to find better jobs and better lives in Cleveland and other northern cities. While they made decent wages, the housing situation proved terrible. Banks made it nearly impossible for blacks to buy their own homes, so they were forced to rent. They lived in garages, sheds, and other places not designed for human inhabitants. Sometimes a home owner

Cleveland, Ohio, is named for the surveyor who founded the community in 1796, Moses Cleaveland. A newspaper printer misspelled Cleaveland as Cleveland in 1831, and from then on, the city was spelled Cleveland.

would rent an eight-room home with just one bathroom to as many as six black families.

Langston attended Central High School in Cleveland. Throughout his high school days, Langston always lived in an attic or basement apartment. At first, he lived with his family, but when Homer tired of the hard work near the hot furnaces in the steel mill, the Clark family eventually moved. By the end of his sophomore year, his mother and stepfather had separated, and Carrie and Gwyn moved to Chicago. Though Langston spent that summer in Chicago with his mother and brother, he was determined to stay in Cleveland during the school year and graduate from Central High School.

Langston liked his high school. Most of the students were children of parents who'd been born in other countries. Langston discovered that these students were less likely to look down on him because he was black. He earned many friends, who nicknamed him "Lang," and he often was invited to their homes. "Everyone adored him," classmate Henry Kraus recalled.

Langston also participated in lots of activities and was elected to many class offices. He took his studies seriously enough to be named at least once to the academic honor roll. He continued writing poetry and found an audience for his work in the school's magazine, the *Belfry Owl*. He also joined the track squad, which earned great success. His relay team twice won the city championship. In his senior year, he edited the school's yearbook.

During the summers, though, he was struck again by the reality of prejudice. No matter how hard he tried, Langston found it difficult to secure a job. But he always found something. The first summer, he ran a dumbwaiter at a department store. The second summer, with his mother in Chicago, he worked as a delivery boy. He also learned that he wasn't welcome in every part of the city he had been so excited to see. Langston remembered:

> The first Sunday I was in town, I went out walking alone to see what the city looked like. ... I wandered too far outside the Negro district ... and was set upon and beaten by a group of white boys, who

said they didn't allow niggers in that neighborhood. I came home with both eyes blacked and a swollen jaw.

Chicago at the turn of the 20th century was an exciting place for young Langston.

Langston saved the money he earned that summer to pay for his own apartment in Cleveland. Starting his junior year, Langston became totally responsible for himself. Along with going to school and keeping up with his homework and activities, he paid for his own one-room apartment and did all his own cooking. He had to make his own meals, because he couldn't afford to eat in a restaurant.

If he'd thought some of the meals with his grandmother were less than appetizing, he quickly grew sick of the one meal he knew how to prepare—boiled rice and hot dogs.

Langston also continued to write poems. He felt shy about sharing them, which always came with the risk of people saying they didn't like his work. Langston took a chance, however, and started sending his poems to magazines. Many rejection letters followed, but he continued trying to get his work published outside his high school.

Then, in the summer of 1919, Langston received a surprise. A letter arrived from his father, James.

Langston's father, James Nathaniel Hughes Jr.

He was coming to New York on business and would be stopping in Cleveland. He wanted Langston to meet him at the train station and travel back to Mexico to spend the summer with him.

Langston was both shocked and excited. He'd heard next to nothing from his father in 11 years. When he told his mother about the letter, Carrie grew very angry. She didn't want Langston to go so far away, but Langston wanted to learn more about his father. He decided to go. "My father ... represented for me the one stable factor in my life," Langston said. "He at least stayed put."

Unfortunately, Langston found life in Mexico depressing. He had to learn Spanish in order to communicate since few there spoke English. James often left on business and did little with his son that Langston considered to be fun. And Carrie refused to write to her son since she remained angry that he'd left the country to be with a man she now despised. Langston remembered:

> *That summer in Mexico was the most miserable I have ever known. I did not hear from my mother for several weeks. I did not like my father. And I did not know what to do about either of them.*

Adding to Langston's misery was the fact that James had plenty of money but chose not to spend it. Langston grew up often wondering where his next meal would come from. Here, in Toluca, Mexico, his father had enough money to buy the finest foods, but they ate beef and beans day after day. Langston had had enough. When his father left on business, Langston ordered a variety of delicious foods from the shops in Toluca. Courageously,

Stores in Toluca offered a variety of fine goods, but Langston's father refused to spend his money.

Langston charged the items on his father's accounts and told James' cook he'd shoulder any blame his father laid on him upon his return. He figured it would be worth suffering his father's wrath in order to eat something other than beef and beans again. Langston stood ready upon James' return. He said:

> *My father stormed and said I was just like my mother, always wasting money. ... So he would usually make a scene*

*whenever he came home from the country,
sending the cook flying from the kitchen
in tears. But, nevertheless, he would
always eat whatever good things were set
before him.*

Langston and James also fought about Langston's future. Without consulting his son, James decided Langston would learn bookkeeping. Langston wasn't sure what he wanted to be after high school, but he knew it wasn't a bookkeeper. Math proved difficult for Langston, which further frustrated his father. "Seventeen and you can't add yet!" James would yell.

After battling with his father all summer, Langston was thrilled when September came. He would be returning to Cleveland to finish his senior year of high school. On the trip back to the United States, Langston pretended to be Mexican in order to get a sleeping room on the train. Blacks weren't allowed such a luxury.

When the train reached St. Louis, Missouri, Langston had a layover. With no air conditioning on the train, the trip was warm. Langston walked over to a soda fountain to buy himself a cool treat. At the soda fountain, the waiter asked Langston if he was a Mexican or Negro. Langston later recalled the conversation:

I said, "Why?"

"Because if you're a Mexican, I'll serve you," he said. "If you're colored, I won't."

"I'm colored," I replied.

The clerk turned to wait on someone else. I knew I was home in the U.S.A.

He'd get further proof of that as his senior year went by. With the end of World War I, white American soldiers returned home and were looking for jobs. They found them. Blacks who had filled the jobs in the soldiers' absence now discovered themselves fired.

Racism became more obvious in other ways, too. Theaters and restaurants in downtown Cleveland that once allowed black customers began putting up signs that blacks no longer were welcome. Langston began to think maybe his father was right about a black man being able to make a better living in countries other than the United States.

When Langston graduated in June 1920, James asked him to come back to Mexico. Langston still remembered how horrible the previous summer there had been, but James hinted that if Langston visited again, he might pay for his college education. Despite the fact his mother would be angry again, Langston felt he had to go back to Mexico if he ever

wanted to have the money to continue his schooling.

The trip would change Langston's life—but not in the way he expected. ᏓᏬ

As a boy, Langston lived in a number of Midwestern cities, traveling in the summer to Mexico to visit his father.

The CRISIS

APRIL 1923   15 cents the copy

4 BACK TO MEXICO

⤳⟡⤵

Langston felt bad. He loved his mother, but she was angry with him—again. Carrie didn't see the use in a college education. Couldn't he just get a job and help her out more? When he tried to explain that he could assist her more with the kind of job that college would help him get, Carrie wouldn't listen. She stood firm. She was angry at Langston for leaving again and even angrier because he was heading toward her ex-husband for the second time in as many summers.

Just like the last time, Carrie refused to see her son off on his journey. Langston trudged to the train station and boarded alone with no one to hug him or wave goodbye. As the train pulled out of the Cleveland station, Langston hoped the trip would be

The Crisis, founded in 1910 as a civil rights magazine, is one of the oldest black periodicals in the country.

worth the pain. It would. "For my best poems were all written when I felt the worst," Langston said. "When I was happy, I didn't write anything."

It would be a long time before Langston felt good about life again. But out of this period of the blues came some wonderful poetry. "The Negro Speaks of Rivers," written while crossing the Mississippi River, came before his train had even left the United States. The poem was complete within minutes. Langston later said:

One of Langston's earliest influences was the poet Carl Sandburg. Sandburg, too, had grown up poor. He became known for his poems about the common people of the United States.

There are seldom any changes in my poems, once they're down. ... Generally, the first two or three lines come to me from something I'm thinking about, or looking at, or doing, and the rest of the poem (if there is to be a poem) flows from those first few lines, usually right away. If there is a chance to put the poem down then, I write it down. If not, I try to remember it until I get to a pencil and paper; for poems are like rainbows: they escape you quickly.

When Langston arrived in Mexico, he found his father had remarried. Berta Schultz had started as James' housekeeper, but they fell in love and got

married. Langston liked her. She seemed to have prompted a slight change in his father, too. James seemed a little kinder—but not enough to make the summer a pleasant one.

Langston was inspired by the Mississippi River as it ran through St. Louis, Missouri.

Langston waited for his father to talk about college, but James was often away on business and had little time to talk with his son. Langston passed the time writing poems and riding horses. In late July, James finally brought up the subject Langston longed to discuss, though James didn't believe there should be much discussion. James thought Langston should travel first to Switzerland to learn German, French, and Italian. Then he should head to Germany to learn about engineering. When college was complete, Langston could easily find a good-paying job as an engineer in the nearby mines around James' ranch. He had it all figured out.

But Langston was horror-struck. He hated math, and engineering involved a lot of it. He also knew he felt shy about making friends in Mexico because he knew only a little Spanish. How could he go to college overseas and learn in another language?

"The thought of trigonometry, physics, and chemistry in a foreign language was more than I could bear. In English, they were difficult enough," Langston said.

Langston already knew he wanted to be a writer. He suggested that he attend Columbia University in New York City. Though he didn't tell his father this, Langston wanted to go to New York City more to visit Harlem than to go to college. The black community with its jazz and its art held a strong attraction for the young man. "More than Paris, or the Shakespeare country, or Berlin, or the Alps, I wanted to see Harlem, the greatest Negro city in the world," Langston recalled.

James flatly refused to spend his money to pay for Langston to go to any college in the United States. He also doubted Langston could make much money as a writer. In addition, James refused to give Langston money to get back home. He told Langston he'd have to stay in Mexico until he came to his senses.

Angry, Langston decided to make his own money to pay for the trip back to the United States. He began teaching English. First, he taught one of his friends. As others saw how quickly the young man picked up the language, Langston's reputation as a teacher grew, and others wanted to learn, too. Soon, he was contacted by two schools that wanted to hire him. Langston took both jobs, teaching at a girls' school in the morning and a business school later in the day. He said:

> *For the first time in my life, I had my own money to spend in decent amounts,*

Until the early 1900s, most African-Americans lived in the South, but between 1910 and 1920, they began moving north in great numbers. World War I created new jobs in Northern industrial cities, and many blacks headed for Boston, Chicago, and New York City and the promise of a better life. This movement, known as the "Great Migration," brought many African-Americans to Harlem and made the New York City neighborhood the "Black Capital of the World."

to send my mother, and to save. ... All that winter I did not ask my father for a penny. And I knew by summer I would have enough to go to New York, so I began to plan my trip long before the winter was over. I dreamt about Harlem.

W.E.B. DuBois (1868–1963), editor of The Crisis, was an outspoken supporter of rights for African-Americans. He was concerned about the relationship between black and white people and wanted to break down people's stereotypes about black Americans. DuBois strongly opposed the views of African-American educator Booker T. Washington, whom Langston had heard speak as a boy. Washington believed that blacks could advance themselves faster through hard work than by demands for equal rights. DuBois was one of the founders of the National Association for the Advancement of Colored People (NAACP), a civil rights organization.

The money also allowed Langston to take in some of the sights he'd hoped to see but didn't the first time he visited his father in Mexico. Chief among them were visiting Mexico City and experiencing the famous bullfights. Langston loved them. He soaked in the roar of the crowd, the sparkle of the bullfighters' costumes, and the spectacle of it all.

Langston also became a published writer during this time. Two stories about Mexico and a children's play, which he called *The Gold Piece*, were accepted by *The Brownies' Book*, a New York magazine aimed at black children. His first article appeared in January 1921.

The magazine was put together by W.E.B. DuBois and the staff at *The Crisis*, the magazine Langston's Grandma Mary first brought to his attention when he was a young boy. In June, "The Negro Speaks of Rivers" was carried in *The Crisis*, marking

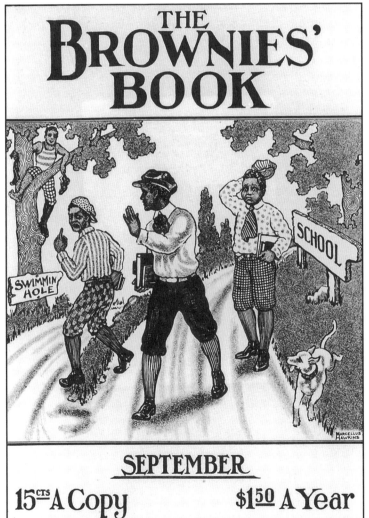

Published by the same organization, The Brownies' Book was a young people's version of The Crisis.

the first time in Langston's life one of his poems was printed in anything other than a school publication.

Though he never got paid by *The Brownies' Book* or *The Crisis*, Langston was thrilled to have his work published.

Finally, James decided his son was serious about Columbia and becoming a writer. He agreed to pay for Langston's education in the United States. Langston couldn't wait to leave.

Although Langston had often been bored and depressed while in Mexico, a close brush with death before his departure was more excitement than he had bargained for. One afternoon, after a day out, he returned to find his father's house swarming with police. They were investigating a shooting that had just occurred. Langston didn't know what to think when he saw the police. He didn't see his father, who'd gone away on business. He didn't see his father's wife, Berta, either. But when he was allowed in the house, he did see a pool of blood in the dining room.

The police told Langston that the German brewmaster in Toluca had stormed into the house with a gun. The brewmaster had fallen in love with Gerta, a young woman who had been visiting at the Hughes house. He thought that she was there to see Langston and was insanely jealous at the thought that she might love another. He shot Gerta three times and then turned the gun on Berta.

The brewmaster felt only half of his work was finished, though. He looked high and low for Langston. In the end, however, he was unable to find Langston, and he ended his bloody rampage. The brewmaster walked to the police station and turned himself in to authorities.

> *Both Gerta and Berta would survive the attack. Gerta spent nearly a year in the hospital and bore scars from the incident. Berta, who was shot in the arm, made a full recovery. The brewmaster was sentenced to 20 years in prison for the shooting.*

Langston thanked his lucky stars he hadn't been home. "Had I arrived at home that afternoon a half-hour earlier, I probably would not be here today," he said.

In September 1921, he began his journey to Harlem. He hoped it would be a journey toward a brand-new life.

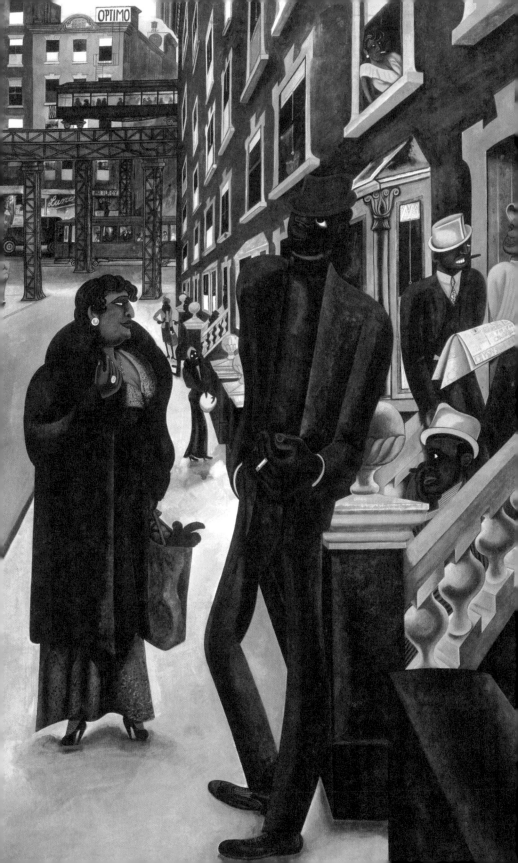

5 A First Look at Harlem

❧⟨×⟩❧

Langston Hughes left Toluca by train and headed to the Gulf of Mexico. There he hopped on a boat that took him up the East Coast to New York.

Arriving in New York City a week before classes were to begin at Columbia, Hughes made his way to Harlem. He said:

> I was in love with Harlem long before I got there. ... Had I been a rich young man, I would have bought a house in Harlem and built musical steps up to the front door, and installed chimes that at the press of a button played Ellington tunes.

One of his first stops in Harlem was the public library, where he was excited to discover books

Edward Burra painted the vibrant culture of Harlem during the time known as the Harlem Renaissance.

In the 1920s and 1930s, Harlem was the center of a great cultural flowering.

about black people. He was also thrilled to see books written by black people.

Harlem in the 1920s was an exciting place to be. Jazz clubs were jumping, and there seemed to be a

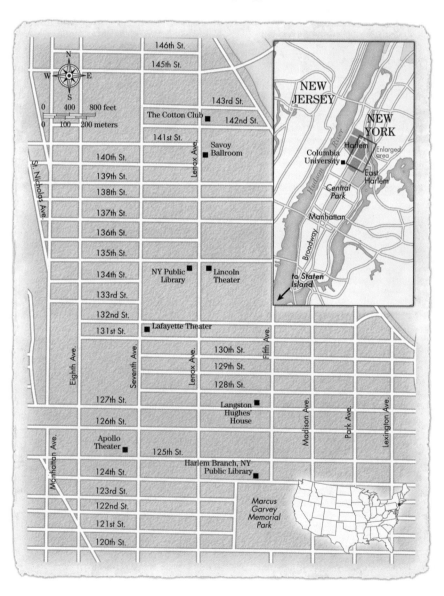

party somewhere every night. The Harlem Renaissance was getting into full swing. Great attention was being paid to black musicians, writers, sculptors, and others with artistic talent. With widespread racism and few economic opportunities for blacks in the United States, the arts remained the one area where they could still flourish.

In 1921, when Hughes first arrived there, Harlem included 127th Street north to 145th Street, and from Madison Avenue west to Eighth Avenue in New York, New York. About 80,000 black people lived in the area. Within a decade, that number would grow to about 240,000.

White people accepted the black artists and also flocked to the clubs in Harlem to hear the catchy music. Most of the black artists, however, were more interested in expressing themselves than in finding the acceptance of a white audience. As more whites took over the black clubs, folks who lived in Harlem resorted to having parties in their own homes. There they could enjoy the hot music, discuss poetry, and be themselves without feeling as if they were being examined by a white crowd.

Hughes said:

> *White people came to Harlem in droves. For several years they packed the expensive Cotton Club on Lenox Avenue. But I was never there, because the Cotton Club was a Jim Crow club for gangsters and*

monied whites. They were not cordial to Negro patronage, unless you were a celebrity like Bojangles. So Harlem Negroes did not like the Cotton Club and never appreciated its Jim Crow policy in the very heart of their dark community. Nor did ordinary Negroes like the growing influx of whites toward Harlem after sundown, flooding the little cabarets and bars where formerly only colored people laughed and sang, and where now the strangers were given the best ringside tables to sit and stare at the Negro customers—like amusing animals in a zoo.

Duke Ellington and his band were popular entertainers of the Harlem Renaissance.

The whites coming to Harlem thought the blacks were happy to have them there. For fear of being harmed, blacks kept their mouths shut. "All of us know that the gay and sparkling life of the so-called Negro Renaissance of the '20s was not so gay and sparkling beneath the surface as it looked," Hughes later said.

Yet Hughes loved Harlem. But he quickly grew to dislike Columbia. Having made his dorm room reservation when he still lived in Toluca, Hughes arrived at Columbia only to hear they didn't have a room for him. However, he knew better. They didn't expect him to be black, and when they realized he was, they pretended not to have a room. Hughes stood up for himself, though, and they eventually gave him the room he had reserved.

But Hughes wasn't very interested in his classes, and it showed in his poor grades. In June 1922, he finished his first year at Columbia and decided it would be his last.

"I didn't like Columbia," he said. "It was too big. It was not fun, like being in high school. You didn't get to know anybody, hardly. The buildings looked like factories."

Hughes undertook the difficult task of writing to his father and letting him know he had quit school. Saying he was going to find a job, Hughes told James he didn't need to send any more money.

Though he was disappointed with Columbia University, Hughes was thrilled to be in Harlem.

"He didn't. He didn't even write again," Hughes said.

Now 20 years old, Hughes did what he really wanted to do—find an apartment in Harlem. Hughes secured a place to stay, but had trouble finding a job, even though lots of jobs were available. Most places didn't want to hire a black man. Hughes said:

> *It was the same in the employment offices. Unless a job was definitely marked COLORED on the board outside, there was no use applying, I discovered. And only one job in a thousand would be marked COLORED. ... Experience was proving my father right. On many sides, the color line barred your way to making a living in America.*

Hughes finally found a job working on a farm on Staten Island. It paid $50 a month and included food and a place to sleep. The work proved hard, though. He rose for work at 5 A.M. and toiled until dark. However, he enjoyed the work and the people who owned the farm. They worked even harder than everyone else.

"We worked hard, ploughing, hoeing, spreading manure, picking weeds, washing lettuce, beets, carrots, onions, tying them and packing them for market," Hughes said.

When the harvest ended, so did Hughes' job. Wanting to see more of the world, he decided to head down to the harbor to see if he could land a job on a ship. The first ship he worked on never left the harbor, but in the spring of 1923, he secured a job helping on a freighter headed to Africa. His adventures overseas were about to begin. 🐟

6 WORLD TRAVELER

Chapter

⁓⦅⨯⦆⁓

Langston Hughes felt a breeze in his hair and the ocean salt on his skin as the S.S. *Malone* headed out toward Africa.

"I was a seaman going to sea for the first time," he remembered, "and I felt that nothing would ever happen to me again that I didn't want to happen. I felt grown, a man, inside and out."

Determined to make a fresh start and create his own adventures, Hughes took his beloved collection of books, and one by one, threw them into the sea. He said:

> *It was like throwing a million bricks out of my heart—for it wasn't only the books that I wanted to throw away, but everything unpleasant and miserable out of my*

Dr. Alain Locke, Hughes' friend and traveling companion, edited a book, The New Negro, that helped define the Harlem Renaissance.

past: the memory of my father, the poverty and uncertainties of my mother's life, the stupidities of color-prejudice, black in a white world, the fear of not finding a job, the bewilderment of no one to talk to about things that trouble you, the feeling of always being controlled by others—by parents, by employers, by some outer necessity not your own. … All those things I wanted to throw away. To be free of. To escape from. I wanted to be a man on my own, control my own life, and go my own way.

He enjoyed the trip to Africa and grew more excited the closer the ship came to the continent's sandy shores. From a distance, Hughes could see the palm trees swaying in the warm breeze.

A hard, heavy wood, mahogany is often used to make furniture. Ranging in color from light tan to a reddish-brown hue, mahogany boasts a variety of grains, or patterns, including wavy or speckled. Some patterns even look like large bird feathers.

The merchant ship carried passengers. It also brought tools, movies, and canned goods to trade for mahogany logs from Africa that would be taken back to the United States.

Hughes' job proved pretty simple. He helped in the kitchen and did some cleaning. Once in Africa, though, local hands were hired to do the work. The ship's regular crew supposedly wasn't used to the heat of Africa, though

Hughes said it was no worse than summer in Chicago. But the regular crew didn't complain, loafing as others did their work.

Hughes visited the coast of Africa in the 1920s as a crewmember on a merchant ship.

Hughes remembered:

> So along the West Coast, life was a picnic for the crew of the S.S. Malone. ... Our supplementary African crew did almost all of the work aboard, and I had an African boy to wash my dishes, set the tables, and make up the rooms for me.

Hughes loved spending time on Africa's shores

and meeting the people. Along with many other souvenirs, Hughes also bought a big, red wild monkey he named Jocko. At first, Jocko bit him every time he came close, but Hughes remained patient and tamed him. He remembered:

> *Then he grew to love me, and wanted to hang on my neck or sleep in my arms. ... But at that stage, out of love for me, he began to bite again, for, whereas formerly he would bite if I picked him up, now he bit if I put him down.*

Nearly every hand on the ship bought either a monkey or parrot to take back to the United States. They even built a special cage on deck to house all the monkeys. Though it was bolted to the ship's deck, the cage broke free during a small storm on the return trip. The frightened monkeys escaped from the cage and ran about the ship, climbing the masts and even messing up important papers in the captain's room. It took the crew two days to finally lure all the animals back to their pen.

Hughes' monkey, Jocko, eventually found a home with Hughes' brother, Gwyn. But their mother, Carrie, was terrified of the animal, and she later sold the monkey to a pet shop.

"My own Jocko was among the last to give up," Hughes said. "But finally he loped chattering into my arms and devoured a prune."

Hughes and the S.S. *Malone* would endure another, worse storm that pushed them off course and off schedule, but eventually they made it back to New York in the fall of 1923. Hughes journeyed to McKeesport, Pennsylvania, to visit his family before returning to New York and finding another job on a ship. This time he was bound for Asia, to visit Constantinople and Odessa.

While loading the ship with supplies, the chief steward fell down a ladder and broke his arm. A new steward was hired to take his place, but this new man wouldn't work with anyone who wasn't white. Hughes was fired.

About a month into its trip, the ship hit a mine left over from World War I. The vessel sank into the Black Sea, and more than half the crew drowned. Had Hughes been on the boat, he likely wouldn't have survived, since he didn't know how to swim. Hughes said:

> *When I read about it, I thought how lucky it was for me that a bag of potatoes had caused a broken arm. And a broken arm, a change in stewards. And that new steward didn't like colored folks.*

It was another close scrape with death, and Hughes lived to tell the tale.

Soon Hughes found another job on a ship bound

for the Netherlands. He liked the trip so well, he went a second time. Upon reaching the Netherlands, however, he decided to see more of Europe and caught a train that was headed for Paris, France.

With only $7 in his pocket, Hughes searched for a place to stay. He knew no one and couldn't understand people, since he did not speak their language. He could read some French, but discovered that understanding it as it was spoken was a different matter altogether.

After asking around for help, Hughes was befriended by a Russian ballerina who also needed a place to stay. They rented a one-room apartment that was so cold they could see their breath in the room. They stuck together, though, and whenever one made some money, they both got to eat. Times grew so tough that Hughes sold most of his clothes to get money for food so they wouldn't starve to death.

Yet he loved Paris. He visited the world-famous Louvre and went dancing at the Moulin Rouge. After a few odd jobs, he was pleased to find steady work as a dishwasher and kitchen helper at a nightclub called the Grand Duc. When other clubs

One of the most famous museums in the world, the Louvre contains many great treasures, including the Venus de Milo and the Mona Lisa. The Louvre boasts about eight miles (13 km) of galleries and more than 1 million pieces of art.

A French poster advertised the popular Moulin Rouge nightclub.

closed for the night, the Grand Duc remained open. Hughes stayed all night listening to some of the finest black musicians of the time jam until the morning light.

Hughes also fell in love with an English girl named Mary. The two talked about marriage, but

Mary's father wouldn't hear of it. She had money, and Hughes had nothing. Mary's father forced her to return to England. Hughes would never marry.

In the spring of 1925, business at the Grand Duc turned sour. To save money, the owner decided to close the nightclub from July until September, when things usually picked up. Rather than finding a short-term job for the rest of the summer, Hughes traveled with some friends to Italy.

While in France, Hughes had met Howard University professor Dr. Alain Locke. The professor was interested in using some of Hughes' poems in a publication he was putting together. The two met again in Venice, Italy. They got along well and enjoyed each other's company. Locke had money and took Hughes to visit museums and eat at fancy restaurants. Hughes enjoyed these touristy activities, but he always felt more interested in spending time with the common people. He often took off on his own to see how most people really lived in Italy.

Hughes took care to protect

Dr. Alain Locke (1885–1954) emerged as one of the principal voices of the Harlem Renaissance, a movement he influenced through the publication of The New Negro. Published in 1925, Locke edited this collection of stories, poems, and essays by black writers. He played a major role in promoting the careers of black writers and artists and encouraging serious critical review of their work.

what little he did have—a few dollars and his passport. Using a safety pin, he fastened his money and passport to the inside of his coat. Aboard a train back to Paris, he decided to take a nap. When he awoke, his passport and money were gone.

Hughes couldn't cross the border into France without a passport. He had no money and no documents to get a new one, either. So, when he got off the train in Genoa, he looked for jobs in the harbor.

It didn't take long for Hughes to grow hungry. He said:

> *Sometimes I was so hungry I would stand in front of a bakery window or a store show case and wonder how I could steal something to eat and not get caught and locked up. But I never had the nerve, nor the ultimate necessity of stealing, for something always seemed to turn up just when I was the hungriest, so that I didn't starve to death.*

Hughes felt his only hope was to join the crew of a ship traveling to the United States. Many turned him down, though, because he was black. Finally, he found a ship's captain who would grant him passage to New York if he worked for him. Hughes couldn't wait to be back in Harlem. ❧

THE WEARY BLUES

BLUES

by
LANGSTON HUGHES

7 A POET IS DISCOVERED

❧⟿❧

In November 1924, Hughes landed in the United States—about 10 months after he first arrived in Paris. His mother and brother now lived in Washington, D.C., and Hughes went to join them.

Washington, D.C., felt much like the South, Hughes thought. Racism was common. He said:

> *Negro life in Washington is definitely a ghetto life and only in the Negro sections of the city may colored people attend theaters, eat a meal, or drink a Coca-Cola. Strangely undemocratic doings take place in the shadow of 'the world's greatest democracy.' In Europe and Mexico I have lived with white people, worked and eaten and slept with white people, and no one seemed any the worse for it. In New York*

Hughes' first book, a collection of poetry called The Weary Blues, *was published in 1926.*

I have sat beside white people in theaters and movie houses and neither they nor I appeared to suffer. But in Washington I could not see a legitimate stage show, because the theaters would not sell Negroes a ticket. I could not get a cup of coffee on a cold day anywhere within sight of the Capitol, because no 'white' restaurant would serve a Negro. I could not see the new motion pictures, because they did not play in the Negro houses.

Hughes had changed a great deal in his travels. He now felt ready for college, but he didn't have the resources to go. Hughes hoped to put some money away, but an emergency always ended up draining his savings. He knew his father would laugh at him if he knew of his situation. As in his most difficult, worry-filled days in Europe, Hughes poured his heart into poetry.

"I didn't like my job, and I didn't know what was going to happen to me, and I was cold and half-hungry, so I wrote a great many poems in the manner of the Negro blues and the spirituals," Hughes said.

Finally, Hughes got a break. While working as a busboy at the Wardman Park Hotel, he learned that the poet Vachel Lindsay would be giving a reading at the hotel. Hughes had admired Lindsay's work since he was in high school, and he was determined to take advantage of the opportunity. He copied down three of his poems and waited until the poet entered the dining room. Hughes managed to slip his poems next to Lindsay's plate and then quickly retreated to the kitchen, awkwardly mumbling his admiration for the poet. From a distance, Hughes watched as Lindsay read the pages, but he didn't see a reaction.

Vachel Lindsay (with his nephew), was famous for his dramatic poetry readings.

American poet Vachel Lindsay (1879–1931) studied art before turning to poetry. His poetry features strong rhythms and vivid images, but Lindsay was most famous for his dramatic readings of his poems. Lindsay believed that poetry should be performed, rather than simply read, and a number of his works include stage directions. Lindsay traveled the country, often exchanging drawings and performances of his poetry for food and shelter.

A huge surprise awaited Hughes when he picked up the next day's paper. He saw the news story. Lindsay had discovered a busboy poet! Lindsay had even read some of Hughes' poems at the poetry reading he had given the previous evening.

When Hughes arrived at work, reporters were waiting to interview him and take his picture. In addition, Lindsay had left a package of books for Hughes, as well as a note of encouragement. Hughes was flying high.

Soon after, Hughes earned first prize in *Opportunity* magazine's first literary contest. He entered several poems, including one he wrote on a ship in New York's harbor titled "The Weary Blues," which proved to be the winner.

Hughes traveled to New York to collect his $40 prize. At the banquet, he saw Carl Van Vechten, an author and critic whom he'd met earlier at an NAACP party in Harlem. Van Vechten asked Hughes if he had written enough poems yet to create a book. When Hughes said yes, Van Vechten asked Hughes to send them to him. Van Vechten loved the poems so much that he submitted them to his publisher. The result was Hughes' first book of poetry, *The Weary Blues*, published in 1926.

Other publications, including *Vanity Fair* and *New Republic* magazines, started buying Hughes' work. He also won an Amy Spingarn Prize for his work and was invited to tea at Spingarn's home.

Hughes talked with Spingarn about his dream to attend Lincoln University, near Philadelphia, Pennsylvania. Lincoln was the oldest black university in the country. He wanted to study history and psychology and learn more about the world. He was eager for knowledge, reasoning that the more he understood about the world and its people, the better his poetry would be. He just didn't see how he'd ever scrape together enough money to continue his education.

The answer came in a letter around Christmas 1925. Spingarn liked Hughes and saw his potential. She offered to pay for Hughes' college education. Hughes remembered:

> *It was the happiest holiday gift I've ever received. My poems had caused me to meet her. My poems—through the kindness of this woman who liked poetry— sent me to college. So at the mid-year I entered Lincoln, and remained there until I received my degree.* ❧

8 SPREADING HIS MESSAGE

❦

This time around, Hughes loved college, but he missed the city. On weekends, he'd head to Harlem where he could listen to jazz and talk with other writers and artists.

Then, in the spring of 1927, Hughes received invitations to read his poems at Fisk University in Nashville, Tennessee, and at a conference in Texas. He accepted both generous offers. He worried a little about reading in the South, though. To his relief, Hughes discovered Fisk University to be a very welcoming place. He said:

> *My visit there was a delightful one. ...*
> *For the first time I stood before a large*
> *audience of my own people, reading my*
> *poems, and I was thrilled, because they*

Hughes (second from left) enjoyed spending time with local citizens when he visited the Soviet Union as a reporter.

> *seemed to like those poems—poems in which I had tried to capture some of the dreams and heartaches that all Negroes know.*

A flood canceled the Texas conference, but Hughes still received a fee. He used the money he had earned to tour the South, including camps that housed people displaced by the flooding Mississippi River. Hughes traveled to Memphis, Tennessee, Vicksburg, Mississippi, and Baton Rouge, Louisiana. In New Orleans, his curiosity led him into drugstores and voodoo shops that sold "magic" medicines.

"I bought some Wishing Powder and I think it brought me luck, because the next day, quite unexpectedly, I found myself on the way to Havana," he said.

While watching a crew unload bananas from a boat in New Orleans, Hughes had noticed another vessel that appeared to be nearly ready to take off. He asked if they needed any kitchen help, and they did. Hughes was on his way to Cuba. "It was just what I wanted," Hughes said, "a short trip that would still allow me a week or so in New Orleans on the return before having to go North to college," he said.

The following year, Hughes could afford to spend his summer vacation writing rather than finding another job. An elderly and wealthy white woman named Charlotte Mason offered Hughes $150 a month in exchange for the opportunity to offer her input on Hughes' writing. With her support, Hughes worked on a novel, based loosely on his experiences of growing up in Kansas.

In the spring of 1929, Hughes had completed his novel—and graduated with honors from Lincoln

Hughes' mother, Carrie, joined him to celebrate his 1929 graduation from Lincoln University.

University, as well. Looking back on his college experience, Hughes said:

> Maybe everyone is sentimental about his college days. Certainly I loved Lincoln. My years there were happy years, jolly and full of fun. Besides I learned a few things. And I wrote Not Without Laughter.

In 1931, Hughes' novel, *Not Without Laughter* won the Harmon Gold Award for Literature. He used the $400 prize to travel with his friend Zell Ingram.

In Florida, they stopped to visit Bethune-Cookman, a college established by black educator Mary McLeod Bethune. That evening, Hughes talked with Bethune about his future.

"Before I went to bed I sat for a long time on the front porch talking to Mrs. Bethune, motherly and kind and wise as she was toward me, a very puzzled young man," Hughes said.

Bethune pointed out the hope Hughes gave to students who heard his readings and lectures.

Mary McLeod Bethune (1875–1955) worked to improve educational opportunities for African-Americans. In 1904, she opened a school for African-American girls that later became Bethune-Cookman College. As director of the Division of Negro Affairs of the National Youth Administration, Bethune was the first African-American woman to head a federal agency.

He was living proof that dreams come true for black people, too, and that not all poets were white. She suggested he add to his income from writing by touring the country and giving readings and lectures. Hughes followed her advice.

Hughes started his tour in October 1931, and it wasn't without controversy. A new poem Hughes wrote caused a sensation when it was printed in an unofficial school newspaper of an all-white university in Chapel Hill, North Carolina, before his visit. The poem, "Christ in Alabama," expressed some of the anger Hughes felt about the unfair imprisonment of several black boys wrongfully accused of attacking two white women.

The school honored its commitment to host Hughes' reading, but he was put in a smaller room than originally planned. Fear of violence led to the posting of police outside the reading. Hughes said:

> *The theatre of the University of Chapel Hill was packed to the doors the night I read my poems there, and special police were on guard to prevent trouble since considerable pressure had been put on the University to cancel my lecture. Courageously, the University refused to do so.*

When Southern newspapers picked up the story about the poem and the trouble in Chapel Hill, other white schools in the South declined to be stops on his tour. Still, plenty of other places were even more excited to hear him, and his tour continued through Texas, New Mexico, Arizona, and California.

Awaiting him in California was a telegram with another opportunity. A Russian film-production company wanted him to write dialogue for a movie it planned to produce about the life of blacks in the

Hughes and writer Dorothy West were among the group of black artists who traveled to Russia to make a movie.

United States. Never one to turn down an opportunity to travel, Hughes signed on to the project.

While the movie was never completed, Hughes got the chance to travel to the Soviet Union and see how blacks were treated there. Once the movie project died, Hughes took a job traveling through the countryside as a reporter. He sold his articles to Russian publications, which paid him well.

After his adventures in the Soviet Union, Hughes traveled to Japan and China. In Shanghai, on China's coast, Hughes was appalled to see how foreigners had brought their Jim Crow laws to this country, too. Hughes was barred from staying at a "white" YMCA and couldn't enter British and French clubs. He reflected, "But fortunately, as everywhere in the world, there were white people ... who did not approve of color lines."

Hughes took in as much of the atmosphere of Shanghai as he could. He watched black entertainers perform in nightclubs. He visited racetracks, markets, and amusement parks. He also visited a large textile factory where he saw how many of the country's children were treated like slaves.

Finally, after being away from the United States for 15 months, he caught a Japanese ship bound for San Francisco, California, where more adventures awaited him. ✿

DEFENSAR **MADRID**
ES
DEFENSAR **CATALUNYA**

9 WAR REPORTER

✎⟊⟊✎

Already a poet, novelist, and reporter, Hughes continued to seek out new challenges. He had become an activist for a number of social and political causes, which offered him plenty of material for a new collection of stories he was writing. Stories in *The Ways of White Folks* centered on the ways in which white people controlled black people. Published in 1934, it was well-received and for a time allowed Hughes the financial freedom to stay in one place and devote himself to writing.

That summer, Hughes' father, James, died, and Hughes traveled to Mexico for the reading of the will. Though his father left him nothing, this time his experience in Mexico was a happy one. He was broke and hungry, but that was a familiar situation.

Posters helped both sides win support during the Spanish Civil War.

THE WAYS OF WHITE FOLKS

STORIES BY

LANGSTON HUGHES

The gritty short stories in The Ways of White Folks *were popular with readers.*

He enjoyed living as he once had in Europe—listening to music, writing poetry, and spending time with other artists. He even translated his poems into Spanish. Nevertheless, Hughes returned to the

United States at the end of the summer.

One fall day in 1935, he discovered that *Mulatto*, a play he'd written six years earlier, was in rehearsals and would open on Broadway. The play dealt with some of the struggles people of mixed ancestry faced. Few black writers ever had a play produced on Broadway, and Hughes was thrilled at his opportunity.

Hughes felt the theater provided a great way to reach people with his message of equality for all. In addition to writing plays, he created his own theater companies in Cleveland, Harlem, Los Angeles, and Chicago. His poems and short stories continued to be published in magazines and books, as well. But in the spring of 1937, everything else took a back seat to what was to become one of Hughes' biggest challenges—war reporter.

The Afro-American, a Baltimore, Maryland, newspaper, hired Hughes to write articles about black Americans serving in the International Brigade during the Spanish Civil War. The war had broken out the previous July after many of the country's army officers revolted against the Republican

The theater in which Mulatto *opened had a segregated seating policy, which Hughes successfully protested.* Mulatto *became a great success on Broadway. It ran for a year in New York City, setting a performance record for a play by a black playwright that would not be broken for 24 years.*

Mulatto *was a popular production and held a Broadway record for many years.*

government. Thinking they'd quickly gain power, the officers planned to put a dictator in place. They didn't count on the patriotism of the common people, though, who revolted. During the course of the Spanish Civil War, about 3,200 Americans would fight for the freedom of Spain, and about 1,800 would die for the cause.

Hughes was greeted in Spain with the sound of nearby bombings. In Madrid, he could see flashes from enemy guns. He learned to ignore the noise by playing jazz—he always brought his music with him.

The children of Madrid and their will to remain happy and active touched Hughes' heart. It wasn't unusual to see youngsters playing in big holes created by bombs that recently had fallen from the sky. "The will to live and laugh in this city of over a million people under fire, each person in constant danger, was to me a source of amazement," he said.

Reporting in a war-torn country proved dangerous, but not as dangerous as joining a tour group, as Hughes discovered when he visited University City, where the lines of battle were drawn.

"Several times in Spain I thought I might not live long," Hughes said. "One of those times when I felt my end had come was at University City."

Against his better judgment, Hughes joined a group of tourists visiting University City. A large hat worn by one of the women in the group drew gunfire. The woman was uninjured, but the bullet grazed Hughes.

In December 1938, Hughes felt it was time for him to leave Spain. He had written every story he could think of, and his presence did nothing but deplete already short supplies. Other reporters had already left the capital. "I knew it was time for me to

American author Ernest Hemingway (right) also worked as a reporter during the Spanish Civil War.

be leaving, too, but I hated to quit the city I had grown to love," he said.

As he crossed into France, Hughes pondered the meaning of countries and borders:

> *What a difference a border makes. ... On one side of an invisible line, food; on the other side, none. On one side, quiet in the sunlight; on the other side the dangerous chee-eep, chee-eep, chee-eep that was not birds, the BANG! of shells, the whine of sirens, and the bursting of bombs over*

crowded cities. I stood alone on the platform that bright December day and looked down the valley into Spain and wondered about borders and nationalities and war. I wondered what would happen to the Spanish people walking the bloody tightrope of their civil struggle.

Back in the United States, Hughes worked to establish a uniquely black theater in Harlem. By the time his Suitcase Theater was well-established, the Spanish resistance was defeated and a new era of rule in Spain had begun.

German dictator Adolf Hitler and Italian dictator Benito Mussolini assisted those seeking to replace Spain's Republican government with a dictatorship. As the two dictators called for the bombing of Spanish cities, rumors flew that the two men were practicing for something bigger. The rumors proved true when World War II erupted in 1939.

10 THE FINAL YEARS

❦

Through the years, Hughes continued to write. In 1940, he published his autobiography, *The Big Sea*. During that decade, Hughes also wrote a column for the *Chicago Defender* newspaper. In 1943, he used this column to introduce the character Jesse B. Semple, known as "Simple." Through Simple, Hughes used humor and common sense to spread the message of equality. Eventually he compiled three books' worth of Simple stories. Today, these books have been translated into many languages and are enjoyed throughout the world.

Hughes enjoyed combining his talent for writing with his love of music by working on operas and musicals. In 1957, he wrote the lyrics and text for a musical based on the character of Simple. The

Those who knew Hughes remember him as a friendly, gentle man who was optimistic about the future.

musical, called *Simply Heavenly*, was performed in New York City and Washington, D.C., as well as in Europe. That same year, he published *I Wonder as I Wander*, the second book about his life. He also wrote several children's books, as well as a history of the NAACP for adults. Hughes' work didn't bring him wealth, but it did bring him joy. He wouldn't stop writing until his health suddenly failed him.

In 1966, Hughes wrote about Simple for the last time. Hughes believed people had become so bitter over racial issues that they could no longer understand or appreciate Simple's gentle kind of humor.

Hughes had lived with pain before, but by March 1967, he really didn't feel well. In fact, his body hurt. Through most of that month and the next, he suffered with the pain, but it wasn't bad enough to drive him to seek a doctor's help. Hughes never liked going to the doctor and had put off visits to the clinic in the past. Having lived most of his life with little money, Hughes didn't want to spend what little he did have at the doctor's office. But when the pain woke him on the night of May 6, he knew he had to seek help.

The doctor found Hughes suffering from infections and other problems, though he didn't believe any of them would prove too serious. Hughes tried to keep his hospital stay quiet and managed to keep most of his friends away. The friends who did know

Hughes was hospitalized believed nothing serious was happening.

On May 12, Hughes underwent surgery for the first time in his life. The procedure—to remove a small, noncancerous lump—was expected to be simple, and Hughes made it through the surgery with flying colors.

The second day after the operation, however, Hughes' health began to fail. His temperature rose, and he complained of terrible pain. The doctors didn't know what was wrong or how to help him. They tried everything they could think of, but it wouldn't be enough. To everyone's horror, Hughes died May 22, 1967, at 10:40 P.M. Only a nurse stood by his side.

Hughes' death was announced on the front page of the *New York Times* the next morning. Friends couldn't believe he was gone—they hadn't even known Hughes had been ill. They'd seen him at recent parties and other get-togethers. He'd masked his pain well.

On May 25, Hughes' friends crowded into a large room at the Benta Funeral Chapel in Harlem to say their final goodbyes to the man they loved. But just like Hughes, the funeral service would prove to be one of a kind. Hughes wanted his funeral to celebrate his life, not to mourn his death. A friend read Hughes' final words:

Tell all my mourners
To mourn in red—
Cause there ain't no sense
In my bein' dead.

A jazz trio also set up to play at the funeral, a request made in Hughes' will. Hughes had even picked the song they were to play at the end of the service—"Do Nothing Till You Hear from Me." He chose it as a joke to amuse his beloved friends.

The impact Hughes made in his 65 years could not be measured. He touched the lives of countless people who searched for their voices—and perhaps later found them through writing.

During his life, Hughes encouraged others to be true to themselves. He taught students that good writing comes from their own experiences. He told them:

> *You will find the whole world just outside your doorstep even if, seemingly, there is nothing there but the concrete sidewalk and a water plug. You will find the world in your own eyes, if they learn how to see, in your heart if it learns how to feel, and in your own fingers if they learn how to touch. What your fingers transfer to paper—if you are able to make yourself into a writer—will grow and grow and grow until it reaches everybody's world.*

Hughes enjoyed children and wanted them to grow up in a world where they could be anything they wanted.

Through his many poems, stories, musicals, plays, and novels, Langston Hughes was true to himself. He wrote about his experiences as an African-American in a language that was true to his roots. Innovative but straightforward, bluesy but optimistic, Hughes' work broke ground for black writers everywhere, and his influence is felt in the words of many artists writing today. ࠕ

HUGHES' LIFE

1909

Moves to Lawrence, Kansas, to live with his grandmother

1902

Born February 1 in Joplin, Missouri

1900

1903

Brothers Orville and Wilbur Wright successfully fly a powered airplane

1909

The National Association for the Advancement of Colored People (NAACP) is founded

WORLD EVENTS

1916

Chosen as class poet; moves to Cleveland, Ohio

1915

Moves to Lincoln, Illinois, to live with his mother

1919

Spends the summer in Mexico with his father

1915

1916

German-born physicist Albert Einstein publishes his general theory of relativity

1919

World War I peace conference begins at Versailles, France

HUGHES' LIFE

1921

Publishes his first poem, "The Negro Speaks of Rivers," in *The Crisis* magazine

1920

Graduates from high school; writes "The Negro Speaks of Rivers" while on the train to Mexico

1922

Moves to Harlem, New York City

1920

1920

American women get the right to vote

1922

The tomb of Tutankhamen is discovered by British archaeologist Howard Carter

WORLD EVENTS

1926

Starts classes at Lincoln University; publishes his first book of poetry, *The Weary Blues*

1929

Graduates from Lincoln University

1923

Begins working on ships that take him to Africa and the Netherlands; later visits Paris, France

1925

1923

Aeroflot, the largest airline in the world, is founded in Russia

1926

Claude Monet and Mary Cassat, well-known impressionist painters, die

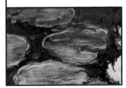

HUGHES' LIFE

1935
Play *Mulatto* opens
on Broadway

1937
Covers the Spanish
Civil War for *The
Afro-American*

1935

1933
Nazi leader Adolf
Hitler is named chan-
cellor of Germany

1936
Civil war erupts
in Spain

1939
German troops invade
Poland; Britain and
France declare war
on Germany; World
War II (1939–1945)
begins

WORLD EVENTS

1940

Publishes his first autobiography, *The Big Sea*

1957

Simply Heavenly, Hughes' musical about the character Simple, is performed

1967

Dies at Polyclinic Hospital in New York City on May 22

1960

1953

The first Europeans climb Mount Everest

1967

The first heart transplant is attempted

NICKNAME: Lang

DATE OF BIRTH: February 1, 1902

BIRTHPLACE: Joplin, Missouri

FATHER: James Nathaniel Hughes (?–1934)

MOTHER: Carrie Mercer Langston (1873–1938)

EDUCATION: College degree from Lincoln University in Pennsylvania (attended one year at Columbia University)

DATE OF DEATH: May 22, 1967

PLACE OF BURIAL: Hughes was cremated.

In the Library

Hill, Christine M. *Langston Hughes: Poet of the Harlem Renaissance.* Springfield, N.J.: Enslow Publishers, 1997.

Hughes, Langston. *The Collected Works of Langston Hughes.* Dianne Johnson, ed. Columbia: University of Missouri Press, 2001.

Hughes, Langston. *Selected Poems of Langston Hughes.* New York: Vintage Books, 1990.

Hughes, Langston. *Short Stories.* New York: Hill and Wang, 1996.

Rau, Dana Meachen. *The Harlem Renaissance.* Minneapolis: Compass Point Books, 2005.

Rhynes, Martha E. *I, Too, Sing America: The Story of Langston Hughes.* Greensboro, N.C.: Morgan Reynolds, 2002.

Look for more Signature Lives
books about this era:

Andrew Carnegie: *Captain of Industry*

Carrie Chapman Catt: *A Voice for Women*

Henry B. Gonzalez: *Congressman of the People*

J. Edgar Hoover: *Controversial FBI Director*

Douglas MacArthur: *America's General*

Eleanor Roosevelt: *First Lady of the World*

Elizabeth Cady Stanton: *Social Reformer*

ON THE WEB

For more information on *Langston Hughes*, use FactHound to track down Web sites related to this book.

1. Go to *www.facthound.com*
2. Type in a search word related to this book or this book ID: 0756509939
3. Click on the *Fetch It* button.

FactHound will find the best Web sites for you.

HISTORIC SITES

Langston Hughes Performing Arts Center
104 17th Ave. S.
Seattle, WA 98144
206/684-4757
To enjoy cultural entertainment and take classes in theater, art, music, and other things Langston Hughes loved during his lifetime

Langston Hughes' Harlem Home
20 E. 127th St.
New York, NY 10035
To see the home where Langston Hughes lived in Harlem

autobiographies
books about the life of the author

downtrodden
experiencing suffering

dumbwaiter
a small elevator used for lifting goods from one
story of a building to another

fledgling
someone who is new to something

mortgage
house payment

physics
the science of matter and energy and how
they interact

racism
the belief that one race is better than another

segregation
the separation of one race from another

stenographer
a person who writes down in shorthand what
another person says and then types out the words

trigonometry
the mathematical study of triangles

turbulent
sometimes violent unrest

Chapter 2

Page 17, line 14: Langston Hughes. *The Big Sea.* New York: Hill and Wang, 1968, p. 14.

Page 18, line 7: Ibid.

Page 18, line 25: Ibid., p. 26.

Page 19, line 18: Ibid., p. 17.

Page 20, line 11: Ibid., p. 12.

Page 20, line 16: Ibid., p. 17.

Page 23, line 9: Milton Meltzer. *Langston Hughes: A Biography.* New York: Thomas Y. Crowell Company, 1968, p. 13.

Page 23, line 26: *The Big Sea*, p. 18.

Chapter 3

Page 28, line 21: Ibid., p. 24.

Page 29, line 8: Ibid.

Page 30, line 14: Ibid., p. 25.

Page 32, line 4: *Langston Hughes: A Biography*, p. 32.

Page 32, line 24: *The Big Sea*, p. 33.

Page 35, line 3: Ibid., p. 36.

Page 35, line 14: Ibid., p. 39.

Page 36, line 7: Ibid., p. 44.

Page 37, line 12: Ibid., p. 45.

Page 38, line 1: Ibid., p. 51.

Chapter 4

Page 42, line 1: Ibid., p. 54.

Page 42, line 12: Ibid., p. 56.

Page 44, line 17: Ibid., p. 62.

Page 44, line 27: Ibid.

Page 45, line 26: Ibid., p. 67.

Page 49, line 13: Ibid., p. 77.

Chapter 5

Page 51, line 7: Arnold Rampersad. *The Life of Langston Hughes, Volume 1: 1902–1941: I, Too, Sing America.* New York: Oxford University Press, 1986, p. 51.

Page 53, line 24: *The Big Sea*, p. 224.

Page 55, line 3: Ibid., p. 227.

Page 55, line 21: Ibid., p. 83.

Page 56, line 1: Ibid., p. 85.

Page 56, line 7: Ibid., p. 86.

Page 57, line 8: Ibid.

Chapter 6

Page 59, line 4: Ibid., p. 3.

Page 59, line 12: Ibid., p. 98.

Page 61, line 5: Ibid., p. 105.

Page 62, line 6: Ibid., p. 120.

Page 62, line 24: Ibid., p. 122.

Page 63, line 20: Ibid., p. 139.

Page 67, line 12: Ibid., p. 143.

Chapter 7

Page 69, line 7: Ibid., p. 206.

Page 70, line 20: Ibid., p. 205.

Page 73, line 22: Ibid., p. 219.

Chapter 8

Page 75, line 12: Ibid., p. 285.

Page 76, line 13: Ibid., p. 291.

Page 76, line 21: Ibid., pp. 291–292.

Page 78, line 2: Ibid., p. 303.

Page 78, line 19: Langston Hughes. *I Wonder as I Wander.* New York: Hill and Wang, 1993, p. 6.

Page 79, line 19: Ibid., p. 46.

Page 81, line 15: Ibid., p. 249.

Chapter 9

Page 87, line 9: *Langston Hughes: A Biography*, p. 215.

Page 87, line 16: *I Wonder as I Wander*, p. 357.

Page 87, line 28: Ibid., p. 384.

Page 88, line 5: *Langston Hughes: A Biography*, p. 217–218.

Chapter 10

Page 94, line 1: Ibid., p. 258.

Page 94, line 20: Ibid., p. 250.

The Academy of American Poets Web site.
http://www.poets.org/poets/poets.cfm?prmID=84

Barksdale, Richard K. *Langston Hughes: The Poet and His Critics*. Chicago:
American Library Association, 1977.

Hughes, Langston. *The Big Sea*. New York: Hill and Wang, 1968.

Hughes, Langston. *I Wonder as I Wander*. New York: Hill and Wang, 1993.

Jemie, Onwuchekwa. *Langston Hughes: An Introduction to the Poetry*. New
York: Columbia University Press, 1976.

Meltzer, Milton. *Langston Hughes: A Biography*. New York: Thomas Y.
Crowell Company, 1968.

Modern American Poetry Web site.
http://www.english.uiuc.edu/maps/poets/g_l/hughes/hughes.htm

Rampersad, Arnold. *The Life of Langston Hughes, Volume 1: 1902–1941: I,
Too, Sing America*. New York: Oxford University Press, 1986.

Rampersad, Arnold. *The Life of Langston Hughes, Volume 2: 1941–1967: I
Dream a World*. New York: Oxford University Press, 1988.

Brenda Haugen started in the newspaper business and had a career as an award-winning journalist before finding her niche as an author. Since then, she has written and edited many books, most of them for children. A graduate of the University of North Dakota in Grand Forks, Brenda lives in North Dakota with her family.

Image Credits